A Picture Book of

ARCTIC ANIMALS

Written and Illustrated by Kellie Conforth

Troll Associates

Library of Congress Cataloging-in-Publication Data

Conforth, Kellie.
    A picture book of arctic animals / by Kellie Conforth.
        p.   cm.
    Summary: Describes a variety of arctic animals, including the harp
seal, polar bear, snowy owl, and collared lemming.
    ISBN 0-8167-2144-0 (lib. bdg.)   ISBN 0-8167-2145-9 (pbk.)
    1. Zoology—Arctic regions—Juvenile literature.   [1. Zoology—
Arctic regions.]   I. Title.
QL105.C66   1991
599.09091—dc20   90-44896

#10668

2

HARP SEAL

A mother harp seal has no trouble finding her baby in a crowd. Each seal *pup* has its own special smell and makes a crying sound that tells its mother exactly where it is.

Seal pups are sometimes called *whitecoats* because they are covered with soft, pure white fur. But by the time they are 4 weeks old, they have gray fur, just like their parents do. By this time, the pups are old enough to go out on their own.

Harp seals spend most of their time swimming in the cold arctic waters, looking for fish to eat. A thick layer of fat, called *blubber*, keeps them warm. A baby seal is born without blubber. As it drinks its mother's milk, which is very rich in fat, a layer of blubber soon forms on the pup's body.

POLAR BEAR

The polar bear is often called "The King of the Arctic." It can weigh up to 1,600 pounds and has no real enemies, except for people.

Even though it is very heavy, a polar bear can walk across very thin ice. It spends most of its life hunting seals on the ice. Polar bears are also very good swimmers. Their thick, oily fur keeps them warm and dry, even in the freezing arctic waters.

A female polar bear usually gives birth to 2 *cubs* during the winter. They stay warm and cozy in a den deep under the snow until spring comes. Then it's time to go back onto the ice, so the mother bear can teach her cubs how to hunt. Cubs usually stay with Mom until they are about 2 years old.

SNOWY OWL

The snowy owl is one of the few birds to live in the *tundra* (the frozen, treeless area that covers most of the Arctic) all year long. It is also one of the few owls to hunt in the daytime. Most owls are *nocturnal*, which means they are active only at night. But in the Arctic, the sun doesn't set all summer long! So the snowy owl must look for its favorite foods—lemmings and birds—while the sun is out.

COLLARED LEMMING

This chubby little animal has 2 coats of fur. In the summer, its fur is brown and yellow. In the winter, this dark fur falls out and is replaced by an all-white winter coat. White fur helps the lemming hide in the snow.

A lemming's fur is not the only thing that changes when winter comes along. Its feet change, too! Hard pads grow on its paws, making them longer, and its claws grow longer, too. These changes make it easier for the lemming to dig *burrows*, or tunnels, through the snow.

ARCTIC WOLF

Most wolves dig shelters called *dens*, but the arctic wolf can't. The ground where it lives is frozen and too hard to dig in. So this wolf must make its home in rocky caves.

Like other kinds of wolves, arctic wolves live in groups called *packs*. 6 or 7 wolves usually make up a pack. One male is the leader. Every year, one of the females gives birth to about 6 pups. All the members of the pack take turns guarding the baby wolves and teaching them to hunt hares, seals, birds, musk ox calves, and even caribou.

RED FOX

The red fox lives in the southern part of the Arctic. Unlike many arctic animals, its fur stays red all year long. In winter, its coat becomes so thick that the fox can sleep in the snow without feeling cold. Even the bottoms of its paws are covered with fur to keep the fox warm.

ARCTIC HARE

An arctic hare's fur is usually white all year long. But when the 5 or 6 baby hares are born in late June, they are covered with gray fur. This helps the babies, called *leverets*, hide against the rocks and the ground, so they are not easily seen by their enemies.

The arctic hare can weigh up to 12 pounds. Its powerful back legs help it hop to escape from wolves and the other animals that hunt it.

ROCK PTARMIGAN

Like many arctic animals, the rock ptarmigan changes color with the seasons. In summer, this bird's feathers are reddish brown and black. These colors match the rocks and grass. In winter, the bird's feathers turn white like the snow. These color changes help the ptarmigan hide from its many enemies, including the arctic wolf and the arctic fox.

The rock ptarmigan spends little time flying. When it is in the air, it is an easy target for hawks and snowy owls that like to eat it. Instead, the ptarmigan stays close to the ground, looking for plants and berries to eat.

PEARY CARIBOU

The smallest kind of caribou is named after Robert E. Peary, who discovered the North Pole. Large herds of caribou are always on the move, searching for arctic willow, moss, and other plants to eat. They use their sharp front hooves to paw through the snow to reach their tasty food.

Even though it is a strong animal, the Peary caribou must always be on the lookout for danger. Wolves love to eat caribou, and the sight of a wolf will send the herd running away as fast as it can.

MUSK OX

A thick, shaggy fur coat protects this huge mammal in both winter and summer. It shields the ox from the icy wind and snow in the winter, and keeps off biting insects in summer. Herds of musk oxen roam the Arctic, their heavy hooves breaking through the ice that covers the plants and moss they like to eat.

Packs of wolves often attack musk oxen, trying to kill a calf o two. The oxen protect their young by forming a tight circle around them and threatening th wolves with their long, sharp horns.

16

WALRUS

The walrus is very clumsy on land, so it spends most of its time swimming. Its heavy skin and thick layer of blubber keep the walrus warm in the freezing ocean. When it does come ashore, the walrus likes to sleep on the rocky beaches.

A male walrus, called a *bull,* can weigh up to 2 tons. They eat up to 100 pounds of food every day. The walrus feels along the ocean floor with its muzzle and whiskers, then sucks clams, snails, and worms into its mouth. Its long tusks aren't used for eating. Bulls use them to fight with each other to see which walrus is the strongest.

KILLER WHALE

For a long time, people thought that these fast-swimming mammals were ferocious man-eaters. That is how they got their name.

But killer whales, or *orcas*, as they are sometimes called, do not eat people. They feed mostly on fish, and sometimes eat dolphins, seals, and sea lions, too.

Killer whales live in family groups of about 6-50 members. These groups are called *pods*. The young calves stay with their parents all their lives. A male can live to be 50 years old. Females can be up to 100 years old!

Killer whales are very smart. They "talk" to each other by making clicks, whistles, and screaming sounds. Each pod has its own special calls.

PUFFIN

Most birds *migrate*, or travel to warmer places, when winter comes. But many puffins stay in the Arctic all year long. They are excellent divers and swimmers. Their webbed feet act like paddles to help them swim. And a puffin's large colorful beak is useful for catching tasty fish to eat.

CANADA LYNX

This furry cat is the only member of the cat family that lives in the Arctic. Its thick coat keeps it warm. And fur covers the bottom of its broad, flat paws, which act like snowshoes. This helps the lynx move quickly over the snow, hunting hares and weasels.

ERMINE

Few arctic animals are as busy as the little ermine. It rushes around, looking for small rodents and birds to eat. Its slender body makes it easy for the ermine to chase its prey into narrow tunnels.

Ermines are a kind of animal called a *weasel*. In summer, the ermine's fur is brown. But in the winter, it turns white. Only the tip of its tail stays black all the time.

DALL SHEEP

The grass and other plants that cover the hillsides of northern Alaska are the perfect food for the Dall sheep. It is the only pure white sheep in the world. Male sheep, or *rams*, use their large, curved horns when fighting over female sheep, or *ewes*. The sound of their horns crashing together can be heard for miles.